Simple Acts of Friendship

Heartwarming Stories of One Friend Blessing Another

NORMAN ROCKWELL

Text by Margaret Feinberg

Guideposts®

CARMEL, NEW YORK 10512

Simple Acts of Friendship
Text Copyright © 2004 by Margaret Feinberg
This Guideposts edition is published by special
arrangement with Harvest House Publishers.

Library of Congress Cataloging-in-Publication Data
Feinberg, Margaret, 1974–
   Simple acts of friendship / [paintings by] Norman Rockwell; text by Margaret Feinberg.
       p. cm.
   Includes bibliographical references.
   ISBN 0-7369-1092-1
  1. Friendship—Religious aspects—Christianity. I. Rockwell, Norman, 1894-1978. II. Title.
   BV4647.F7F45 2004
   241'.6762—dc22

                                2004001055

The author, Margaret Feinberg, can be reached at P.O. Box 2981, Sitka, AK 99835, by emailing mafeinberg@juno.com, or visit www.margaretfeinberg.com.

Artwork and compilation of artwork Copyright © 2004 by the Norman Rockwell Family Entities. Reproduced by the permission of the Norman Rockwell Family Agency Inc. All images appear courtesy of the Curtis Publishing Company.

Design and production by Koechel Peterson & Associates, Inc., Minneapolis, Minnesota.

Scripture quotations are from the HOLY BIBLE, NEW INTERNATIONAL VERSION®. NIV®. Copyright ©1973, 1978, 1984 by the International Bible Society. Used by permission of Zondervan. All rights reserved.

Printed in the United States of America.

•

The best relationships...
are built up like a fine lacquer finish,
with accumulated layers
made of many little acts of love.
GILBERT AND BRADSHAW

•

A Friend's Suggestion

Friendship is the source of the greatest pleasures, and without friends even the most agreeable pursuits become tedious.
ST. THOMAS AQUINAS

Clyde Forsythe was a celebrated cartoonist who had worked in the newspaper world long enough to recognize good drawings from bad. Unlike some others, Clyde was always straightforward and honest when someone asked him what he thought. And fellow artists who had the tough skin to take his assessment not only found constructive criticism but an encouraging friend.

Clyde watched with curiosity when one of his artist friends painted "100%" in gold at the top of his easel. The artist explained that he wanted everything he did to be 100% as good as it could possibly be. After each painting, the artist asked Clyde to rate the work, and Clyde faithfully gave a rating, always trying to be honest and helpful.

One day Clyde noticed his friend was particularly discouraged, and so he went out of his way to encourage the young man. "Why don't you do a cover and show it to the *Saturday Evening Post?*" he challenged.

Clyde proceeded to convince the young artist that his work was not only good but good enough for one of the country's top publications. The young artist went to work the next morning. And in March of 1916, the young artist—Norman Rockwell—sold his first painting to the *Saturday Evening Post.*

He who loves a pure heart and whose speech is gracious will have the king for his friend.
THE BOOK OF PROVERBS

"I'd Like You to Meet…"

Our friends interpret the world and ourselves to us, if we take them tenderly and truly.
AMOS BRONSON ALCOTT

•

Jan had grown up with Laura and knew her well. Together, they had done things that most teenagers did in the 1960s— borrow the family car, head to a '50s-style drive-in, and enjoy a Coke at the local hang out.

Even throughout college, Jan and Laura maintained their friendship. After college, Jan watched as most of her friends got married and started families. But not Laura. She was working as a teacher and decided to head back to graduate school at the University of Texas for a degree in library science.

Jan often wondered when Laura would settle down. Whenever Laura came home for a visit, Jan would try to set her up with a young man she knew. But Laura made it clear that she wasn't interested in a relationship. Her time at home was for family and friends.

Laura held her ground for several years. In 1977, however, she finally agreed to meet the young man at one of Jan's barbecues. Thanks, in part, to Jan's simple act of friendship, Laura and George fell in love and married within three months.

Some may have questioned or even showed a bit of concern for such a short engagement, but it's obvious that Laura made a good choice in marrying George Bush—a man who would go on to become the forty-third President of the United States.

We are sometimes made aware of a kindness long passed, and realize that there have been times when our friends' thoughts of us were of so pure and lofty a character that they passed over us like the winds of heaven unnoticed; when they treat us not as what we were, but as what we aspired to be.
HENRY DAVID THOREAU

Love Has Thirty-Six Inch Doors

Hold a true friend with both your hands.
NIGERIAN PROVERB

•

When my parents' friends Kent and Diana Busing decided to move to western North Carolina, they knew they didn't want to do it alone. So they joined two other couples who had been lifelong friends and decided to purchase a large parcel of land together and build their homes on the property.

By the time I finally paid my first visit, they had just completed the massive project. As I walked through my friends' home, I was taken by the thoughtful architecture and design. The kitchen was roomy, the living room seemed ready for guests at any time, and the doorways were extra large.

"I really like your doorways," I commented.

"Oh, those are for Darby," Kent responded.

"Why did you design your home for someone who doesn't even live here?" I asked.

"Because while we were building our home, our neighbor Darby began suffering from multiple sclerosis," Kent explained. "Within months she was using a wheelchair. Most doors come in a small standard size. For our doors to always be open to Darby, we need them to be thirty-six inches, which is standard for wheelchair accessibility. They're more expensive, but they're worth every penny. Darby feels comfortable coming over and visiting whenever she wants—even when we're not here."

I cast another glance at the frame of the door and realized that true friendship requires not only expanding your heart, it means expanding your life and even your home to accommodate those you love.

Love one another deeply, from the heart.
THE BOOK OF 1 PETER

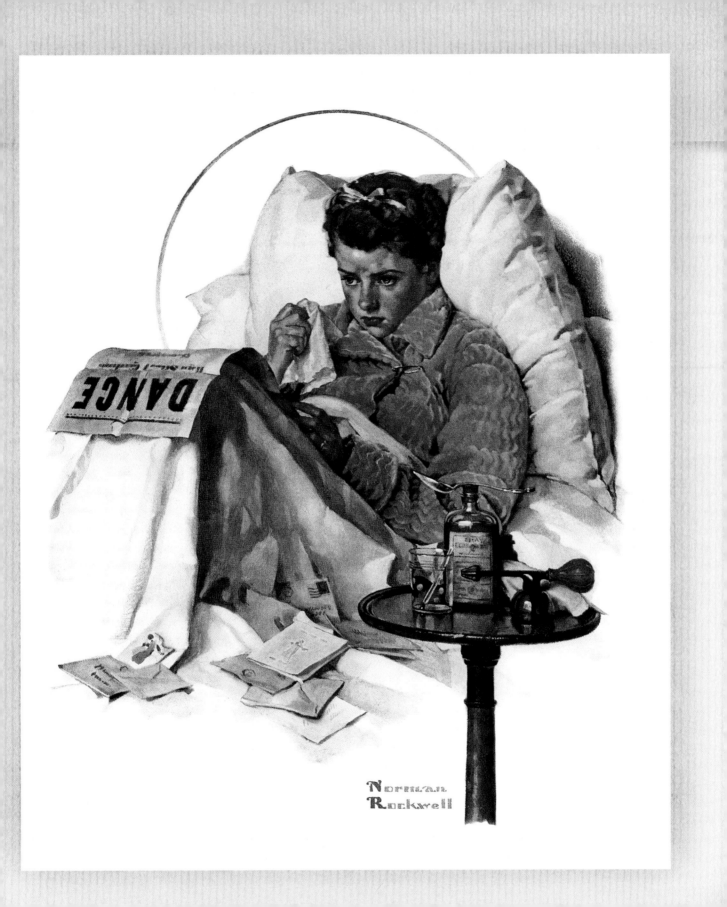

Fathering Friendships

The greatest sweetener of human life is friendship.
JOSEPH ADDISON

•

In 1990, Gary Erickson was living in a rented garage in California with his skis, bicycle, climbing gear, and dog named Boomer. During the days he worked part-time designing bike seats and was a half-owner in a local bakery. But on nights and weekends, the 33-year-old bachelor was on his bike—training, racing, and competing.

When Gary had to resort to four wheels, he drove a 1978 Datsun 510—purchased for a mere $375. "Thank God for duct tape," Gary recalls. "Eventually, the bike rack was more valuable than the car itself. I sold the car to my friend Clem for $10, who gave it to our friend Jay a few years later for free. That car just kept on going and going."

Gary had a great friendship with his parents, but his father, Cliff, was more than a little concerned about his son's future. Would he ever settle down, get married, and land a "real" job?

The answer emerged after a 175-mile bike tour with his buddy Jay. Gary was munching on an energy bar and reached the point where he couldn't take another bite. He knew there had to be a better-tasting alternative.

Two years and countless recipes later, Gary created his own energy bar right out of his mom's kitchen and named it after his father. Since its humble beginnings in 1992, Clif Bars Inc. has grown into a multi-million dollar business with brands including Clif Bar, LUNA bar, and Mojo Bar.

The good news is that Cliff doesn't have to worry about his son anymore. Not only does he have a successful company, but he's also happily married with three kids. And even with a hectic schedule, Gary still manages to maintain a strong friendship with his mom and dad—he has breakfast with his parents every Thursday morning.

Letters of Long-Lasting Friendship

Can miles truly separate us from friends?

RICHARD BACH

•

While in junior high school, Mary Lynne Rapien was an active member of her Girl Scout troop. She sold cookies door-to-door, but one particular set of customers did more than purchase a few boxes. They opened a door to a lifelong friend.

Mary Lynne recalls three elderly women who bought ten boxes of cookies. When she went to deliver them, Mary Lynne was asked if she'd like to write one of their relatives, a teenage girl named Rosemarie living in Germany. The year was 1952.

Their friendship grew through the correspondence, and at the age of twenty, Mary Lynne flew to meet her foreign friend.

"I flew to Europe and took a train to Germany to visit my friend," Mary Lynne recalls. "We shared four wonderful days. We took a boat ride down the Wasser River where we saw castles built into the mountainside."

The two continued to write, and in 1969, they were given the opportunity to meet again—this time with both of their families. In 1983, they were also able to reunite.

Over the years, Rosemarie's children have visited Mary Lynne in the United States and Mary Lynne's grandchildren have spent time visiting in Germany. It's a friendship—which began with letters—that has lasted for more than half a century.

This is the pleasure of corresponding with a friend, where doubt and distrust have no place, and everything is said as it is thought.

SAMUEL JOHNSON

Childhood Friends

A friend loves at all times.
THE BOOK OF PROVERBS

•

Jason's and Aimee's families met in Amarillo, Texas, in 1977. When the parents became friends, so did all of the kids. The two families enjoyed a rich friendship that included camping in northeastern New Mexico during the summer and skiing and sledding in the winters.

Around the time Jason was nine years old, Aimee's dad sledded into a tree and cracked his skull. The families spent days together at the hospital while he recovered.

The parents of both families relied on each other during their children's teen years. Camping and skiing trips continued. More injuries were sustained, albeit less severe, until the year after Jason's high school graduation. During a ski trip to Taos, Jason's father broke his hip in a freak skiing accident, and the families were given yet another chance to bond in the hospital.

"We joke now that our families are no longer allowed to travel together," Jason says.

In 1994, Jason married the daughter of their family friends, Aimee, his lifelong friend.

"I've known her—our families have known each other—since I was three, and she was two. Our set of friends became a family, and we wouldn't have it any other way. We don't know of any other couple who can display a picture of themselves together as little kids. We can. It's the two of us, at a table surrounded by our siblings, on a trip to the mountains in the winter of 1980. We were sledding. No one got hurt."

I do love nothing in the world so well as you...
WILLIAM SHAKESPEARE

Beyond Barriers

Friendships are fragile things and require as much care in handling as any other fragile and precious thing.

RANDOLPH S. BOURNE

•

Lucy was at Home Depot one day, shopping for a ceiling fan, when she heard a commotion. A ten-year-old boy, evidently autistic, was shrieking and throwing himself around wildly in a tantrum. His mother, a slender Muslim woman in flowing robes, had a toddler in her orange cart. She was embarrassed, frantic, and unwilling to leave her toddler to chase after the older child.

Lucy stepped up to the cart and asked, "May I help you? I can watch the little one while you help your son." The woman nodded, "Thank you" and recovered the other child. Lucy learned the woman's name, Adaiya, and that the woman happened to live in Lucy's neighborhood.

When summer came, Lucy began seeing Adaiya at the local pool, and they developed a friendship. Lucy told her about Jesus.

Just before the start of the new school year, Lucy received a note in the mailbox from Adaiya. "We are returning home," the note said. "It will be good to be back with family. But I will always treasure our time in the U.S. because of you. You made me welcome. You were my friend. Because of you, I began to think that Jesus could be a Friend, too."

A few weeks later, Lucy opened the *Washington Post*. Near the end of the first section was a photo of the leader of an Arab nation. Next to him was Adaiya's husband—the new minister of the interior for that Muslim country.

Be imitators of God, therefore, as dearly loved children and live a life of love...

THE BOOK OF EPHESIANS

A Box of Friendship

•

Into a box of friendship,
To ensure that it is strong,
First a layer of respect
On the bottom does belong.
Then to the sides attach,
In the corners where they meet,
Several anchors full of trust,
Devoid of all deceit.
The height of friendship can be measured
By the sides of four,
So make them all a larger cut
And the box will hold much more.
Now fill it up with courtesy,
Honor and esteem,
Understanding, sympathy
And passion for a dream.
Add to that your honesty,
Emotions joy and love,
And since they're so important,
Place them up above.
But leave the box wide open,
So all can see inside,
To learn what makes a friendship work
From the box you built with pride.

AUTHOR UNKNOWN

•

A Literary Friendship

A friend is someone with whom you dare to be yourself.
FRANK CRANE

•

It's strange to think that two of the great writers of the twentieth century were not only contemporaries, they were friends. C.S. Lewis, author of classics such as The Chronicles of Narnia series and *Mere Christianity*, and J. R. R. Tolkien, author of The Lord of the Rings trilogy, enjoyed each other's company immensely.

In fact, Tolkien was one of the keys to Lewis' return to Christianity. Lewis, who had abandoned the faith as a teenager, had a stirring conversation with Tolkien and Hugo Dyson, an instructor at Reading University, over dinner. The conversation lasted until 3 A.M., as they discussed the connection between Christianity and mythology.

After the remarkable conversation, Lewis wrote to a colleague, "I have just passed on from believing in God to definitely believing in Christ…. My long night talk with Dyson and Tolkien had a great deal to do with it."

Long after this fateful evening, Lewis and Tolkien found themselves exchanging ideas, criticism, and applause for each other's works in a long-standing series of meetings known as Inklings. It was a remarkable friendship between two literary greats.

Friendship is born at that moment when one man says to another:
"What! You, too? I thought that no one but myself…"
C.S. LEWIS

A Special Brother, A Special Friend

True friendship is seen through the heart, not through the eyes.
ANONYMOUS

•

On April 24, 1992, my brother Matthew John was born. I didn't think much of it then, but as I look back, he changed me forever.

My brother was born a healthy, happy baby, but as he got older we noticed something different about him. We later learned he was autistic. That means his brain doesn't work normally, that he lives in his own little world.

Matthew has made a major impact on my life, because I learned that not everyone is the same. When I was little and saw a retarded child or adult, I thought he or she was just weird. I didn't know about mental illnesses or disabilities. Now that I know a person like that, I understand and don't stare or make fun of them.

Another thing that Matthew has taught me is how to love people. He has taught me patience. Whenever people give me a hard time, I don't yell at them. I try to work it out, every time.

Even though he has problems that make him different, that doesn't mean that he's weird. I love him. He is my brother and my friend.

Kristen Messina, age 13
Gibsonia, Pennsylvania

Hearts are linked to hearts by God…That friend, given to you
by circumstances over which you have no control, was God's own gift.
FREDERIC WILLIAM ROBERTSON

The Friendship Ball

*A friendship can weather most things and thrive in thin soil—
but it needs a little mulch of letters and phone calls and small silly presents
every so often—just to save it from drying out completely.*

PAM BROWN

•

Every so often, we are given the opportunity to meet someone special, someone we don't want to let go. One of those women in my life is Sheila Frost.

I met her years ago while living in Pensacola, Florida. She rented a home across the street with her husband and older daughter, and their place became a revolving door of warmth, grace, and God's love. Whenever I was having a down moment, I could visit Sheila, sit on her couch—well worn from the many visitors who passed through her door—and be encouraged by her friendship.

Sheila Frost was feisty, funny, and she had a sharp wit about her that made you laugh out loud. A visit with Sheila was nothing less than remarkable. She listened. She asked questions. She encouraged. And most importantly, she loved unconditionally.

Eventually, the day came for me to move away from my sweet, memorable neighbor. I wondered how we would keep in touch. That's when I discovered a friendship ball—a small silver ball with a metal clasp that allows gifts to be exchanged between friends. I gave Sheila the friendship ball before I moved, and since then the ball has bounced back and forth through the mail with all kinds of gifts—everything from chocolate to fuzzy slippers to toenail polish to books and CDs.

The gifts are always fun, but it's the love that's behind each mailing that helps keep our friendship going even after all these years.

It takes a long time to grow an old friend.
JOHN LEONARD

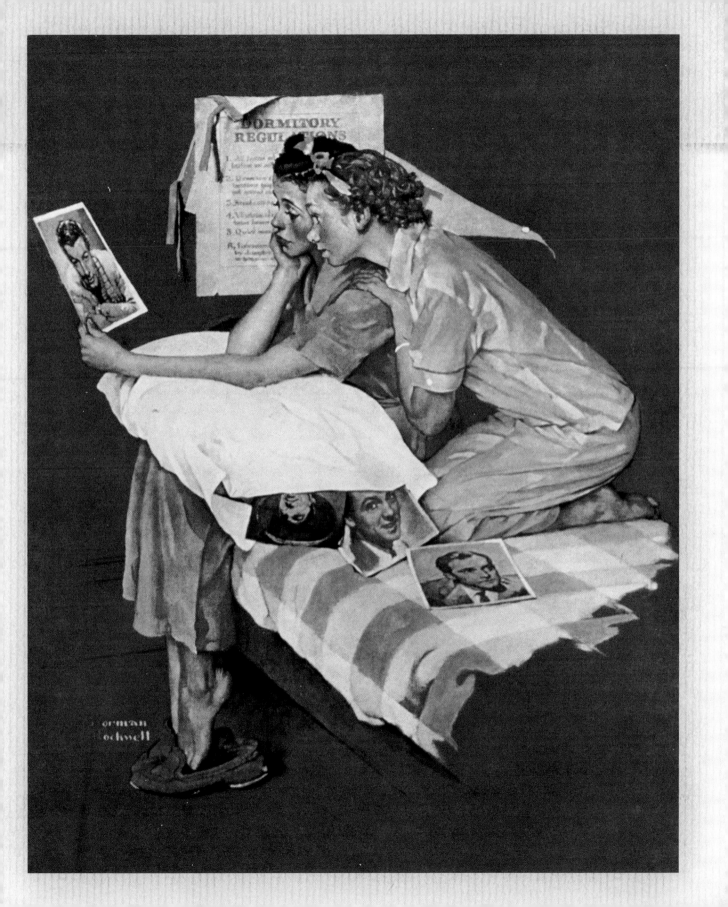

Bread in the Window

Be merciful, just as your Father is merciful.
THE GOSPEL OF LUKE

•

An old story is told about a soldier in the aftermath of World War II, who was walking down a historic street in a foreign country. The landscape was scarred from the many bombings, and those who lived in the region knew it would take years to rebuild. Among the brokenness of the town's streets, the soldier noticed a young boy standing outside a storefront staring in the window. As he passed by, the soldier realized the boy was captivated by something small in the window: a loaf of fresh-baked bread.

The boy was one of countless young children left homeless and possibly orphaned in the wake of the war. With food and supplies scarce in the area, it could have been days since the child had eaten. The soldier took a few more steps, but he just couldn't let the scene go. He turned back, walked into the bakery, and bought two loaves of bread. Then, he walked outside the storefront and gave the young boy one of the loaves—a simple act of friendship. After a quick pat on the head, he kept walking.

As the soldier walked away, he heard the boy ask, "Sir, are you Jesus?"

The dearest friend on earth is a mere shadow compared to Jesus Christ.
OSWALD CHAMBERS

Three Brothers, Three Kidneys

The best time to make friends is before you need them.
ETHEL BARRYMORE

•

In 1973, Rich Salick was driving his Dodge back from college when he began feeling ill. He pulled over and began vomiting. Within 24 hours, Rich lost thirteen pounds and was finally rushed to a hospital where he discovered the cause: kidney failure.

The doctors explained to Rich that he needed a new kidney immediately. Before the young twenty-something could comprehend the news, his brother Phil walked in the room and asked "So, when do we do this?"

With the average kidney transplant lasting between nine and eleven years, the transplant was considered a huge success when Rich's kidney lasted thirteen years before needing another.

In 1986, Rich's older brother Channing gave up his kidney, and when Rich's kidney failed again in 1999, his younger brother Wilson came to the rescue.

Through the extraordinary acts of friendship and kindness of his brothers, Rich was inspired to help others who were less fortunate. Today, Rich Salick has helped raise more than four million dollars for the National Kidney Foundation.

Two are better than one, because they have a good return for their work:
If one falls down, his friend can help him up.
THE BOOK OF ECCLESIASTES

Friendships Throughout Generations

*If we would build on a sure foundation in friendship,
we must love friends for their sake rather than for our own.*

CHARLOTTE BRONTË

•

James Spurgeon was a man ahead of his time. Nearly two hundred years ago, he pastored a congregation of more than 600 with his trademark down-to-earth teaching and tender care. But rather than draw denominational lines between his church and others in the community, he forged friendships with other pastors and church leaders.

In fact, he had a strong friendship with a nearby Anglican rector named Mr. Hopkins. The relationship was so strong, that the two comfortably shared members of their congregations.

James probably never noticed that a young pair of eyes was watching him, but his grandson, Charles was often at his side during the meeting times. The young boy munched on sugared bread and butter at the amiable meetings and learned through his grandfather's acts of friendship that believers should be friends even if they had differences.

When Charles grew up, he followed in his grandfather's and father's footsteps and also became a preacher. In 1854, Spurgeon arrived in London at New Park Street Church, a congregation of 232 members. Thirty-eight years later, the church had more than 5300 members and became the largest independent congregation in the world at the time. Though his church attracted members of parliament and the royal court, some of his contemporaries dubbed him a heretic for his preaching. Yet because of his grandfather's example, Charles Spurgeon managed to maintain surprisingly open and strong friendships with other denominations and their leaders.

*Friendship is something that raises us almost above humanity…
It is the sort of love one can imagine between angels.*

C.S. LEWIS

Love Thy Neighbor

Friends are God's way of taking care of us.
AUTHOR UNKNOWN

•

Building relationships, especially friendships, takes time, intentional effort, and patience. Sherie Henderson, a missionary in Russia, discovered this truth with a woman who lives in her apartment building.

Luba, a woman in the same apartment complex, experienced a terrible tragedy when her son was murdered on the steps right outside the entrance of their building two years ago. Following the tragedy, Sherie saw Luba outside and reached out to her. "We hugged and she cried on my shoulder," Sherie recalls. "We said very little, except that I had heard of her son's death and that I was praying for her."

Luba and Sherie continued to bump into one another every once in a while, and each time, Luba would always kiss Sherie on the cheek and the two would embrace, giving the Russian woman a few moments to cry. Sherie never said much, except that she cared and was praying.

One day Luba asked Sherie, "Why is it that my soul has connected with you even though we rarely see one another and we really don't know one another?" Sherie explained that it is because God Himself causes such precious connections.

More recently, Luba was over for tea. Sherie and her husband were able to help her with a financial need that would enable her husband to have surgery on a broken arm, in hopes that the nerves and use of the hand would be restored.

"It's taken two years to get to this point of trust," Sherie says. "And now we can demonstrate the Lord's personal care for her."

Dear friend, you are faithful in what you are doing for the brothers,
even though they are strangers to you.
THE BOOK OF 3 JOHN

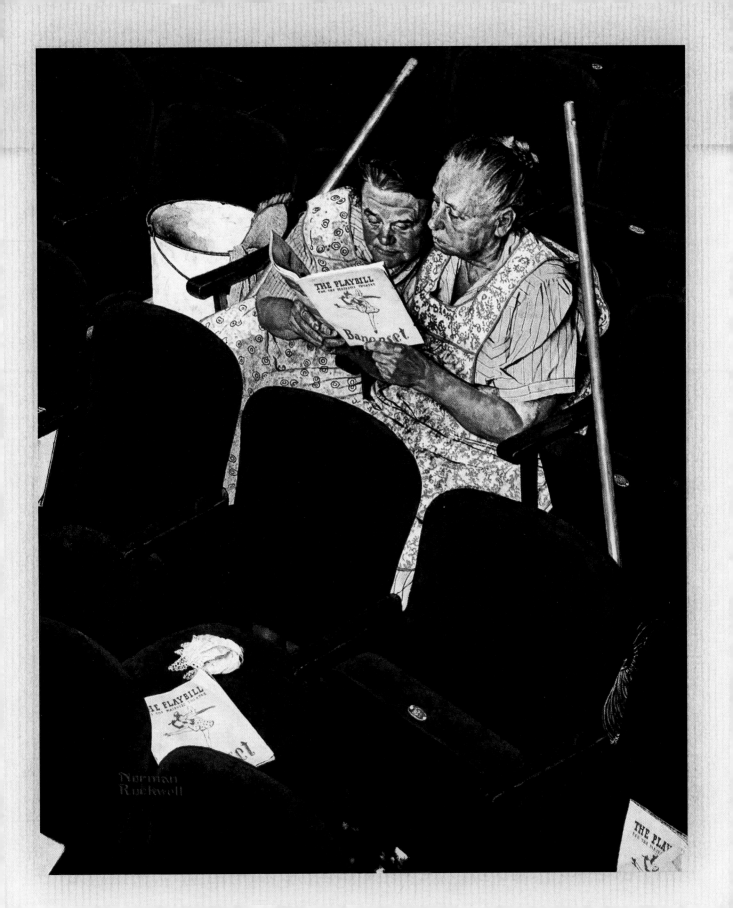

Fighting Friends

Your friends will know you better in the first minute you meet than your acquaintances will know you in a thousand years.

RICHARD BACH

•

Though lanky and awkward at times as a child, Abraham grew into a tall, strong, and lean 185-pound man. Towering above his opponents at six foot, four inches, the twentysomething could outwrestle anyone in his town.

It didn't take long for word to spread about Abraham's skill and strength. A gang from a nearby town challenged him to a match. Their champion was Jack Armstrong, a man whose last name was representative of his power. Word spread about the fight, and people came in from near and far to watch.

Jack took the offensive and rushed at Abraham, who held him off at arm's length. They wrestled for some time before Abraham finally suggested they quit since neither opponent could seemingly win. Jack agreed, and the two became good friends. Little did the youthful Armstrong know he was just one of the many people to be blessed by the peace-loving friendship of a future President of the United States—Abraham Lincoln.

True happiness consists not in the multitude of friends, but in the worth and the choice.

BEN JONSON

Wise Words on Friendship

*True friendship is a plant of slow growth,
and must undergo and withstand
the shocks of adversity before it
is entitled to the appellation.*
GEORGE WASHINGTON

*If you want to win a man
to your cause, first convince him
that you are his sincere friend.*
ABRAHAM LINCOLN

*Friendship is the only cement that
will ever hold the world together.*
WOODROW WILSON

*Meeting Franklin Roosevelt was like
opening your first bottle of champagne;
knowing him was like drinking it.*
WINSTON CHURCHILL

*My friends have made the story of my life.
In a thousand ways they have turned my
limitations into beautiful privileges, and
enabled me to walk serene and happy in
the shadow cast by my deprivation.*
HELEN KELLER

*Sometimes our light goes out but is
blown into flame by another human being.
Each of us owes deepest thanks to those
who have rekindled this light.*
ALBERT SCHWEITZER

*The finest thing of all about friendship
is that it sends a ray of good hope into
the future, and keeps our hearts from
faltering or falling to the wayside.*
CICERO

Unexpected Friendships

Dear children, let us not love with words or tongue but with actions and in truth.
THE BOOK OF 1 JOHN

•

During the filming of *Final Solution*, director Cristobal Krusen says one of the most memorable things that happened on the set was that the staff gathered to pray each day prior to shooting the scenes. "I made it clear from the beginning that attendance at this time of prayer was not required of cast or crew," he recalls. "We had some Christians on the set, but the majority of people were not professing Christians. For those who did join us in prayer, I would always ask them to take the hand of the person next to them, and we would form a circle of prayer."

Initially, attendance was sparse, but then it grew. One day, Krusen was in a rush to get the first scene of the day started, and he skipped the prayer circle in the interest of time. The gaffer, a big, burly man named Mohammed, whose language at times would make a sailor blush, pulled Cristobal aside and spoke to him privately. "Say, boss, aren't we going to have the prayer meeting today?" he asked.

"I looked in Mohammed's eyes," Cristobal recalls. "He was clearly troubled. It turned out that the father of one of his assistants was in the hospital with cancer and wasn't expected to live out the week. We gathered for prayer. I found myself crying as we prayed for the father of this crew member, and the man holding my hand tightest of all was Mohammed."

Sometimes the most profound friendships are developed with complete strangers, whom we have the courage to embrace.

Friends minister to each other, nurse each other. Friends give to each other, worry about each other, stand always ready to help.
STEPHEN E. AMBROSE

Man's Best Friend

The reason a dog has so many friends is that he wags his tail instead of his tongue.
AUTHOR UNKNOWN

•

In 1858, the police constable, John Grays, was buried in Edinburgh's Greyfriars Churchyard. While a number of people attended the funeral, only one friend stayed afterward: Bobby.

Bobby, as you may or may not have guessed, was a dog. He was a Skye terrior and a faithful companion of the police constable. In fact, he was so faithful that he refused to leave his master's graveside. The dog could not be convinced—through punishment, banishment, or treats—to leave the site. Though he might search for food during the day, he returned to the grave each night.

Two stories eventually developed about the dog—which one is true no one really knows. One story suggests that his dog tags were paid for by the Lord Provost, and in another version, the dog was made an actual citizen of Edinburgh, thus protected from canine law.

Either way, Bobby was permitted to stay at the gravesite, where he remained for fourteen years until his death. Today, if you're in Edinburgh—between the George IV Bridge and Candlemaker Row—you'll discover a statue of Bobby commemorating one of the most faithful furry friends who ever lived.

He is your friend, your partner, your defender, your dog. You are his life,
his love, his leader. He will be yours, faithful and true, to the last beat of his heart.
You owe it to him to be worthy of such devotion.
AUTHOR UNKNOWN

Pen Pals from Across the Globe

Letters boost the spirit and bring healing to the soul.
FLORENCE LITTAUER

•

When Diana read about a pen pal exchange in a newsletter, she decided to sign up her ten-year-old daughter Molly. Shortly after, her daughter began exchanging letters with Olena, a girl of the same age who lived in the Eastern Ukraine.

"I'm not sure I had a clear notion of where the USA was, but I knew it was somewhere very far," Olena recalls. "Even if it were a letter from another planet, I couldn't have been more surprised."

Since Olena was still learning English, her mother helped translate the letters before sending them to her new American pen pal. Over the years, the two girls have discussed everything from their schools and families to their cultures and homelands and have exchanged gifts, photos, and souvenirs. Once both families had email access, the pen pal relationship grew even stronger.

In 2003, nine years after the original letter was exchanged, Molly and Olena met for the first time.

As a result of their friendship, Olena says she has decided to pursue a career in international relations. "Our correspondence has given me a broader look at the world around me, and in a way… brought me to where I am now," Olena says.

These pen pals lives demonstrate to us that a little intentional effort—such as letter writing—can help build a rich and rewarding friendship.

When I go to the mailbox each day and rifle through reams of ads and flyers, my heart always unconsciously seeks the handwritten return address of a friend.
ALEXANDRA STODDARD

A Simple Act of Generosity

Friendship is built on caring, sharing, and trust.
AUTHOR UNKNOWN

•

Within a few weeks of their granddaughter's birth, Deanne and Rennie received startling news: their first grandchild had severe heart problems. The baby was airlifted to a hospital in a nearby city, while the parents and grandparents followed.

They experienced an emotional roller coaster during their seven-week stay. After a particularly exhausting day, several of the family members headed to a Red Lobster for a much needed meal and time of relaxation. During the meal, the manager and a staff member named Tracy came over and learned of their story.

The family left, but the story so touched Tracy that she knew she had to do something. With only a bit of information—their hometown and the first name of the child—Tracy and her staff members managed to track down the family and left a message with the natal intensive care ward. When the family returned the call, they discovered the general manager had invited them to a complimentary evening at the restaurant.

A few weeks later, the grateful family returned and were treated with loving care throughout the evening. Before the end of the night, the staff presented them with a giant teddy bear for the infant and promised that funds from the restaurant's next charity drive would be presented to one of the hospital's foundations.

"As a family in another province, we were absolutely swept off our feet with the love and care shown," one of the family members explained. "We have made some lifelong friends with the staff at Red Lobster and think they are exceptional people."

Make every effort to add to your faith goodness...and to brotherly kindness, love.
THE BOOK OF 2 PETER

Sacrificial Friendship

Many people will walk in and out of your life,
but only true friends will leave footprints in your heart.
ELEANOR ROOSEVELT

•

Esther Kim spent much of her life training for the Olympics. She spent many years alongside her childhood friend, Kay Poe, practicing and refining their skills in Tae kwon do.

At the U.S. Olympic trials, Esther and Kay faced each other in an early round. Esther lost the match, but won all her other rounds, which qualified her for the finals.

Meanwhile, Kay won all of her matches, until the fight before the finals, when she dislocated her knee. Esther watched from the sidelines as her friend's knee was painfully reset. Kay managed to stand on one leg and miraculously win the match.

Only one slot was available on the Olympic team, and only two contestants remained in the competition: Esther Kim and her injured friend, Kay Poe. "I looked at her with one good leg against me with two good legs," Esther Kim recalled, "and I said, 'It's not fair!'"

In a courageous act of friendship, Esther forfeited the match so her friend Kay—whose leg would heal by the Olympics—could realize her childhood dream.

"This was our dream, going to the Olympics," Esther said. "I gave her my dream," she added, "but for the first time ever, I feel like a champ."

As I have loved you, so you must love one another.
THE GOSPEL OF JOHN

Notes

"A Friend's Suggestion" is adapted from *Norman Rockwell: Illustrator* by Arthur Guptill (New York: Ballantine Books, 1971) pp. xix–xxi.

"I'd Like You to Meet…" is adapted from *Profile: Laura Bush, wife of Governor George W. Bush* by Jacki Lyden. "Weekend Edition," NPR (Sunday, July 30, 2000).

"Fathering Friendships" is taken from an interview with Gary Erickson on October 16, 2003.

"Letters of a Long-Lasting Friendship" contains quotes reprinted from "The Treasure of a Pen Pal" by Mary Lynne Rapian, *St. Anthony Messenger,* copyright 2001. Used by permission of St. Anthony Messenger Press, 28 W. Liberty St., Cincinnati, OH 45202; 800-488-0488. All rights reserved.

"Beyond Barriers" contains quotes taken from *How People Grow: What the Bible Reveals About Personal Growth* by Dr. Henry Cloud and Dr. John Townsend (Grand Rapids: Zondervan, 2001), pp. 130-131. Used with permission of the publisher.

"A Special Brother, A Special Friend" is taken from "A Special Brother, A Special Friend" by Kristen Messina, *Skipping Stones* (May 1, 2000), p. 31. Used with permission of the publisher.

"Three Brothers, Three Kidneys" contains quotes taken from an interview with Rich Salick on October 27, 2003.

"Friendships Throughout Generations" is adapted from *Charles Spurgeon: Boy Preacher to Christian Theologian* by Kathy Tiggs (Minneapolis: Bethany House Publishers, 1984), pp. 10-11.

"Unexpected Friendships" contains quotes from an interview with Cristobal Krusen on March 19, 2003.

"Pen Pals from Across the Globe" contains quotes taken from "Overdue Rendezvous: Pen Pals Meet Nine Years After First Letter" by Ann Gorman, *State Journal Register* (September 27, 2003), p. 7. Used with permission of the author.

"A Simple Act of Generosity" contains quotes taken from "An Act of Kindness" by Jamie Hall, *Edmonton Journal* (August 29, 2003). Used with permission of the author.

"Sacrifical Friendship" contains quotes taken from "Esther Kim" by Steve Goodier. Posted at www.charityfocus.org (July 20, 2000). Used with permission.